Spiritual Care for Non-Communicative Patients

of related interest

Spiritual Care for Allied Health Practice
A Person-Centered Approach
Edited by Lindsay B. Carey, PhD and Bernice A. Mathisen, PhD
Foreword by Harold G. Koenig, RN, MD
ISBN 978 1 78592 220 6
eISBN 978 1 78450 501 1

Treating Body and Soul
A Clinician's Guide to Supporting the Physical, Mental and Spiritual Needs of Their Patients
Edited by Peter Wells
ISBN 978 1 78592 148 3
eISBN 978 1 78450 417 5

Psycho-spiritual Care in Health Care Practice
Edited by Guy Harrison
ISBN 978 1 78592 039 4
eISBN 978 1 78450 292 8

Art of Living, Art of Dying
Spiritual Care for a Good Death
Carlo Leget
Foreword by George Fitchett
ISBN 978 1 78592 211 4
eISBN 978 1 78450 491 5

Hope and Grace
Spiritual Experiences in Severe Distress, Illness and Dying
Dr Monika Renz
ISBN 978 1 78592 030 1
eISBN 978 1 78450 277 5

Linda S. Golding
and
Walter Dixon

Foreword by
Rabbi Mychal B. Springer

Spiritual Care for Non-Communicative Patients

A Guidebook

Jessica Kingsley *Publishers*
London and Philadelphia

First published in 2019
by Jessica Kingsley Publishers
73 Collier Street
London N1 9BE, UK
and
400 Market Street, Suite 400
Philadelphia, PA 19106, USA

www.jkp.com

Library of Congress Cataloging in Publication Data
A CIP catalog record for this book is available from the Library of Congress

British Library Cataloguing in Publication Data
A CIP catalogue record for this book is available from the British Library

ISBN 978 1 78592 742 3
eISBN 978 1 78450 479 3

Printed and bound in the United States

This guidebook is dedicated to the patients and families who allow strangers in, at the very worst times of their lives.

Contents

Foreword

Rabbi Mychal B. Springer

During my chaplain residency I was assigned to care for patients and families in an intensive care unit (ICU). I remember how much energy it took for me to get myself to the ICU every day. The intensity of illness, the proximity of death, and the difficulty of knowing whether my care was making a difference all made it hard to show up. I cried out to God in new ways as I encountered the unspeakable suffering. I was so grateful for my clinical pastoral education (CPE) educator and peer group—people to whom I turned as I felt overwhelmed and as I sorted through the challenges. With their help I looked at my resistance to being present and discovered the blessings of pastoral presence.

Over the last ten years I have walked students through the challenges of providing pastoral care to people in hospice, many of whom cannot communicate verbally. When Chaplain Linda Golding told me that she was focusing on helping chaplains learn how to provide effective care to non-communicative patients, I arranged for her to come to the Center for Pastoral Education at the Jewish Theological Seminary and conduct a training workshop. Linda joined us at the hospice residence and offered the students a space to articulate their fears and challenges, and receive concrete guidance and support for developing best practices for caring for non-communicative patients. She enlisted the hospice nurses to model their care for us, pointing out the many ways that the nurses engaged the patients, aware that people are listening and responding even when they cannot communicate verbally. The students were deeply grateful and palpably relieved to have a focused session on how to offer this essential care. By receiving this instruction they were then able to disclose the intensity of the fears they were carrying and their profound sense of helplessness.

The training raised up the needs of non-communicative patients and reaffirmed our belief that every person is precious and is worthy of love and care. While the sense of helplessness keeps people defended and at a distance, the cultivation of skills and tools allows us to come close and ease the suffering.

By writing *Spiritual Care for Non-Communicative Patients*, Linda Golding and Walter Dixon have given practitioners a beautiful gift. They share the wisdom that they have acquired through countless visits, and invite us to stand on their shoulders. Their warm, collegial tone offers the reader the opportunity to reflect on all aspects of care and opens up avenues for deepening the spiritual care that we are able to offer those who are not able to ask for it. I am confident that, with the guidance of this book, more people who cannot advocate for themselves will receive life-enhancing care from spiritual care providers who have received the exquisite guidance that this book offers. I wish I had received this book as I embarked on my journey in the ICU back when I began my training, and I'm grateful to have it now.

Rabbi Mychal B. Springer
Director of the Center for Pastoral Education
Jewish Theological Seminary, New York

Preface

The chaplain's work is to listen closely and to bear witness to the circumstances of human existence and resilience. We offer space for the ancient art of storytelling and point out landmarks that can support a patient's recollection of the premorbid self. The pastoral listener helps reveal the meaning in a person's life and experiences, the core and vitality of a being. This intensely creative, personal, and spiritual work takes as many forms as there are human experiences, and usually involves an exchange of communication—body language, eye movement, drawing, music, and the spoken or written word. The chaplain enters a new level of the creative endeavor when confronted with a patient whose comatose state makes the usual modes of communication impossible.

Written for multifaith chaplains and caregivers from all walks of life with a spiritual inclination, this book is a guide to support you as you offer pastoral care to non-communicative patients. It is a hospital-based, hands-on roadmap through the unknown and includes reflective exercises (called ChapTime), role plays, and excerpts from the voices of chaplains who have contributed to this work. The book is divided into the different episodes of a visit with patient, family, and medical team, and can be read in any order—much like the fluid nature of a chaplain's work day and the shifting circumstances in a healthcare environment. The episodes offer different ways to cross the threshold to be with patients who cannot respond because of their comatose state, to be with their families and friends, to model for the medical team what it means to be a chaplain to non-communicative patients, and to seek and share the spirit of the incapacitated patient. In short, they are demonstrations of ways to show and give full dignity to the human being in the hospital bed. You can translate this work to a broad range of non-communicative patients in other types of facilities, but to be clear this book is written from the point of view of adults unable to communicate due to brain injury, sedation, or naturally occurring or medically induced comatose states. You may find you already know some of what is here, so please go to the episodes that attract you.

When a patient is able to express thoughts, needs, or concerns, the chaplain has training and experience to draw on for the dialogue. When the patient is comatose and cannot express these thoughts, needs, or concerns, the chaplain can be at a loss. You can use this book for your own learning or clarification, or to teach students. Included in the Resources is an outline of the didactic given to chaplain interns and residents at NewYork-Presbyterian (NYP) Hospital, as well as medical students and nurses.

The phrase "non-communicative" is used to indicate that the patient is unable to be in dialogue in the ways we usually employ to interact with others—through speech, writing, and non-verbal actions. It is a more broadly descriptive phrase of a patient's condition than "non-responsive," although for the sake of variety you will see both phrases, along with "comatose." Further, "non-communicative" leaves room for the growing scientific work identifying different levels of consciousness and responsiveness among comatose patients.

The general tone of *Spiritual Care for Non-Communicative Patients* is intended to be collegial, inviting, and without reference to specific religious traditions. The guidebook is an exploration in offering spiritual support through humanity and dignity. It is an expansion of a presentation given at the 2016 Caring for the Human Spirit Conference in San Diego. The session attracted a capacity crowd of professional chaplains eager to learn together—a wonderful way to begin a conference!

The most joyful and satisfying part of writing this book has been the opportunity to slow down the process of the didactic and to insert the kinds of reflections and observations we sometimes take for granted.

Responding to a Need

A Quality Improvement Idea

Some years ago, a chaplaincy student mentioned that he did not visit patients in the intensive care units (ICUs) in the hospital unless he received a call or was paged to do so. (Visiting ICUs is a specific part of a chaplain's responsibility in our large, urban hospital.) When asked why, the student replied simply, "I don't know how to provide pastoral care to a patient who is unconscious."

Voice of the Chaplain:

What do I say or do? Can the person hear me? What do I say to the family? What will the medical team think?

Other students expressed similar concerns as well as the desire to shadow the staff chaplains on visits with comatose patients. It became clear that crossing the threshold into the ICU room of a non-communicative patient presented some specific learning and pastoral care opportunities.

Most clinical pastoral education (CPE) programs in the United States offer students the opportunity to shadow staff chaplains during patient visits at the beginning of their training. Often students accompany staff chaplains to presentations or family or hospital committee meetings, to develop a sense of where and how chaplains are involved. Students are quickly encouraged to begin seeing patients on their own, bringing their experiences back to supervision or to their training cohort. Direct supervision, when the CPE educator follows a student during visits, is rare and usually comes towards the end of a training period for evaluation purposes.

It became clear that a didactic on pastoral care with non-communicative patients would benefit from a mixture of teaching and learning techniques, and so an outline was devised: a brief pre-visit questionnaire filled out by each student about their concerns and expectations, followed by shadowing, role play, discussion, a brief post-visit questionnaire about the learning, followed by closing discussion and reflection. In a break from the usual shadowing plan, the chaplains would follow people who spent their days and nights working with non-communicative patients—nurses in the ICUs. We would learn how the nurses engage with their patients and families and adjust as appropriate for pastoral care. The unit patient care directors agreed with the plan and suggested which nurses to approach. We ran into our first problem: most of the ICU nurses were familiar with teaching new nurses practical ICU skills, but not with being shadowed by chaplains. In fact, they were uncomfortable with the idea. Demonstrating task-based skills was typical but being witnessed for their humanity in relationship with another human was new. Before we could begin with the chaplain students, we needed to offer pastoral care to the nurses and speak with them about the goals of the project. The nurses turned out to be eager learners and teachers!

Voice of the Chaplain:

Making the assumption that the person is aware and sentient even if they can't respond.

Very quickly, following initial efforts and evaluation and with the support of the CPE educators, the two-hour "Didactic on Pastoral Care with Non-Communicative Patients" became part of the curriculum for each chaplain intern and resident class. The didactic, led by a staff chaplain, is scheduled once the students are oriented to the hospital and have begun seeing patients, so that it is an additive experience. The training is also offered in nursing home and hospice settings and is adjustable for all professional, student, and patient populations.

The didactic has an immediate impact on students, helping to develop their self-supervision skills and the ability to cross the threshold into ICU rooms as well as into other unknown situations.

How to Use This Guidebook

Gently, Slowly

Each of the episodes of a hospital visit described in this guide stands on its own and can be read or practiced repeatedly as appropriate to your needs and interests. On paper, the order of the episodes follows the path of a chaplain's visit to an intensive care unit (ICU), but the reality is that the orderly path often does not exist. Whatever path you choose, please begin by answering the first part of the brief two-part questionnaire that is part of the didactic. And when you have come to a resting place in the excursion, please complete the second part. (Both parts of the questionnaire can be found in the Resources section at the back of this book.)

ChapTime

Reflective exercises, called ChapTime, are included throughout the episodes to help forward and deepen your experience as a chaplain, and to encourage you to pause to consider rather than feeling the press to move ahead. (They are also listed in the Resources.) The publisher has kindly agreed to leave space for notes so you can write your ChapTime responses while you are reading or while you are in action.

Voice of the Chaplain

Each time the didactic is taught, participants are asked to fill out a two-part questionnaire. A selection of the responses, the Voice of the Chaplain, appear in each episode as commentary to the text. We chose to use these excerpts in place of vignettes or case studies because of the value of peer response. We do not often hear the concerns or triumphs of our colleague chaplains, and we are using the Voice of the Chaplain to help normalize and validate the reader's own experiences. An extended list of Voice of the Chaplain excerpts is included in the Resources section.

Voice of the Chaplain:

Treat as you wish to be treated; stand close to the patient; speak to create a sense of safety.

Who's who?

There are dozens of people involved in the care of an individual patient: nurses, physicians, social workers, care coordinators, nurse practitioners, physician assistants, nutritionists, medical technicians, hospital transporters, environmental workers, food service staff, patient advocates, physical and occupational therapists, speech and language therapists, creative arts therapists, psychologists, child life specialists, medical students, interpreters, administrators, and more. As you work through the guidebook, you will want to add the team members appropriate to your work circumstances.

Voice of the Chaplain:

My greatest concern with an audience is feeling or looking silly as I interact with the non-responsive patients.

Role plays

In the Resources section at the end of the guidebook you will find a collection of role plays to use for teaching and learning. The role plays begin with a brief story line and some instructions, and the roles include family, medical team, a chaplain, observers, and the non-communicative patient. Each participant debriefs the experience of the role play with the patient-player speaking last. The idea of role plays came about out of necessity when a conference presentation was being prepared—in the hospital, it is relatively easy to visit non-communicative patients, but not so easy in a conference presentation. The experience of the role play and the debrief often result in powerful and emotional insights, and role plays became a significant part of the in-hospital didactics.

Prayer

Many people think a chaplain's main role is to pray aloud, and usually in a recognizable form—a lament, a plea, a request, a paragraph of gratitude, or a set religion-specific text. And perhaps you do pray aloud during many of your visits. Over the years, some chaplain students have said that instead of going into the room of the comatose patient, they will stand at the door and say aloud a blessing or a prayer for healing.

> Voice of the Chaplain:
>
> Is there anything to offer besides prayer? How do I know their beliefs?

This action serves to continue the notion of prayer as the primary intervention, and the work ahead in this guidebook will help evaluate that intervention and change the perception for ourselves and for those who see us walking down the hallway and say, "Chaplain, this patient could really use prayer." The comatose patient cannot, in this moment, articulate what emotional and spiritual support would look or sound like.

> Voice of the Chaplain:
>
> How do I support patient autonomy?

Be curious about your drive to pray aloud.

Alone

The extensive who's who of the care team is divided up into shifts and rotations necessitating sophisticated communication and information-sharing techniques. The interaction and interconnectedness of the team is critical to the success of the common goal of caring for, curing, and healing the patient (and the family), and the team becomes an extended family complete with emotional responses and needs.

Even in a large and collegial department, the chaplain tends to be alone while building and maintaining membership in many different teams throughout the day, providing care, to be sure, but also acting as a flexible connection between the team members, patients, and families. We walk with people in the hallway, sit with colleagues in the cafeteria, and we may be well-integrated into the hospital and feel fully seen and embraced. In the end, though, we are largely alone in this building designed to provide refuge and healing. We are one of the hosts.

When I (LSG) walk through the halls of my large, urban hospital, I frequently think of the huts and booths built to celebrate the Jewish holiday of Sukkot. The booth is built of lightweight material with a semi-permeable roof designed to provide covering for shade yet openness for rain to fall in. The cement and steel hospital is like this hut, full of life both fragile and temporary, joyful and sorrowful, permeable and providing for different needs throughout the day and night. This guidebook will take you into the places of the greatest uncertainties in the hospital, and you may find yourself alone, while in the company of others. The booth will protect you even as it exposes you, bringing your vulnerabilities close to the surface.

1 | In the Hallway

The Long Walk

In the middle of the journey of our life I came to myself within a dark wood where the straight way was lost.

Dante Alighieri, *The Divine Comedy,*
Inferno Canto 1 (trans. Charles Lyell)

On any given day, a hospital chaplain may attend interdisciplinary rounds and speak with social workers, nurses, doctors, nursing attendants, physical and occupational therapists, speech and swallow specialists, unit assistants, food service staff, and members of the housekeeping and security teams. In each case, the chaplain both provides and receives information about patients and families.

Referrals can come to the chaplain from any member of the hospital team. In the case of the non-responsive patient, a referral for spiritual support is often given for the family or friends. Although there is a general agreement that such a patient can hear, the referral is rarely for the patient. Given this general agreement, and supporting literature (see Resources), this guidebook is based on the premise that the patient can hear something—but just what that is must wait until the patient can tell us.

ChapTime 1

Recall a conversation when you were told you did not
need to visit a comatose patient because he or she would
not be able to engage with you. How did you feel?

Let's go onto the intensive care unit (ICU). The first stop is the hallway—a
nurse looks at you and wonders who you are coming to see. A family
turns away from you. Or towards you. There is the usual soundscape
made up of beeps and bells from the life-sustaining machines, the
ringing of phones and pagers, the buzz of talk among the medical team
and floor staff, and the one-sided cell phone conversations of family
members or friends. These sounds and unspoken emotions surround a
patient without directly including him or her. Depending on the time
of day, the patient may be alone in the room or surrounded by family
or friends who are talking among themselves or staring at the bedside
monitors. Perhaps the patient is being examined by the medical team
or being cared for by the nurse.

ChapTime 2

Stand still. Which sounds go with which
piece of medical machinery?

ChapTime 3

What is the story being told by bedside monitors?
What is the tone of the conversations around you?
Any smells? What do you think? How do you feel?

The hallway is a metaphor for aspects of chaplaincy—journey, transition, connection, entry, leaving. It can also be an obstacle. There are many opportunities to provide meaningful pastoral care in the hallway of any hospital, but these do necessarily lead to the patient.

Voice of the Chaplain:

Are there responsive patients who need me more?

ChapTime 4

What concerns do you have about visiting a non-communicative patient?

If you are responding to a referral, you know which room to enter. But if you are visiting the unit on your rounds, you will need to make choices. A few questions to open the process:

How do you decide which room to enter?

What draws you into a room, but keeps you from entering?

Do you walk through the unit inquiring of needs?

Do you look into each room before returning to enter a room?

2 | Entering the Room

The Patient Is Alone

No act of kindness, no matter how small, is ever wasted.

Aesop, The Lion and the Mouse

Preparing to cross the threshold

Crossing the threshold into a patient's room can be a challenge for any chaplain. We hold the expectations of those who see us entering and those already in the room, as well as our own.

When entering the room of a non-communicative patient who is alone, the chaplain carries the responsibility of being a witness to the patient's circumstances. In addition, the chaplain is expected to model behavior for the care team, demonstrating how to interact and connect with a human being who cannot respond. This modeling can be seen by the care team or described after the encounter. As the chaplains learned from shadowing the nurses in the didactic described earlier, there is much to teach, learn, and share.

ChapTime 5

What expectations of yourself do you carry in the moment of entering a patient's room? And when standing in the room?

Some practical structure

When does the pastoral visit begin?

As in other situations, the visit begins at the moment the chaplain decides to enter the room. A check with the nurse or physician can reassure the chaplain that the patient's stability will not be impacted by a stranger's visit. You will want to ask about touch, language, preferred name, and any relevant information about family or medical condition.

What about introductions? How does the chaplain explain the purpose of the visit?

A nurse can use the patient's name and detail the physical care to be provided; the examining team or radiology technician outlines the coming plan of action. The chaplain's introduction is similarly supported by any information we have already acquired. Our introduction comes out of our authentic and open-hearted curiosity, tempered by the weight of our own levels of concern or unease, and those we carry from the care team.

Voice of the Chaplain:

Will my presence raise scary or painful thoughts?

Each chaplain has a collection of introductions to use, and choosing the best match for each patient room is part of the art of chaplaincy: a neutral tone, yes, but with what content for a non-communicative patient alone in a room? See what you think of these and add your own:

- "Good morning! I am Chaplain Walter; I heard you are a skier and wanted to let you know about the remarkable snowfall we had last night."

- "Greetings Mr. James! I am Chaplain Sherri and I am visiting patients today to offer a meditation for healing. I will sit by your side for five minutes and meditate."

- "Hola Señor Álvarez! Mi nombre es Padre José. Vengo a visitarte esta tarde."

- "Good afternoon! My name is Linda and I am the chaplain here today. I heard you arrived here this morning and wanted to keep you company for a few minutes."

- "Hello Ms Macy! I am Ellen, the chaplain. I see you have a picture of the Virgin Mary pinned to your pillow. She is keeping you company today, and I will join you both for a few minutes."

We acknowledge information about time of day, demonstrate a little knowledge about the patient, take pastoral authority, and do our best to practice cultural sensitivity in these opening words.

Crossing the threshold

As you stand or sit with the patient, notice the machines and monitors, if any, and their sounds. Consider the disruptive or soothing nature and whether your speech or physical proximity seems to impact anything. If the patient is not intubated, perhaps the breathing rate changes. Research tells us that a non-communicative patient may respond to sound or body heat.[1] The chaplain provides both. Look around the room and notice what you see:

Cards	Drawings	Items indicating religious connections
Books	Photos	
Magazines	A stuffed animal	Newspapers (what date?)
Bible or other sacred/ religious book	Coffee cups	Nothing except medical materials

1   Abbas, M., Mohammadi, E., and Sheaykh Rezayi, A. (2009) 'Effect of a regular family visiting program as an affective, auditory, and tactile stimulation on the consciousness level of comatose patients with a head injury.' *Japan Journal of Nursing Science* 6, 1, 21–26.

Tjepkema-Cloostermans, M.C., Wijers, E.T., and van Putten, M.J.A.M. (2016) Stimulus induced bursts in severe postanoxic encephalopathy. *Clinical Neurophysiology* 127, 11, 3492–3497.

Notice the language and dates; see if you can identify the patient in a photo. These items help you build a narrative, offering clues to the person in front of you and to the chaplain's possible interventions. Consider reading from a card or a well-thumbed page of a book of poems, or the prayer card attached to the pillow.

Or maybe there is music playing from the TV or from a personal device. These details may be rich in personal meaning and connection. The chaplain has a chance to help bring the meaning and connection closer to the surface by mentioning them to the patient and to the care team, and so bringing a fuller sense of the patient's humanity. And remember—if there is nothing in the room, this does not automatically mean that there is nothing to know or no one cares. Be imaginative and curious!

Voice of the Chaplain:

Overcoming the "Am I talking to myself?" anxiety.

ChapTime 6

Consider the items that would help a care team begin to get to know you if you were the patient.

If there is narrative-making material at hand in the room, the chaplain can enter into a dialogue with the material as the representative of the patient. The dialogue may be about telling the patient what is in the room and wondering who brought it, rather than making assumptions that these items are a full expression of the patient's identity. If you see the name of the patient in a book or on a magazine address label, that gives you a little more certainty of connection.

If there is no narrative-making material from outside the hospital, there are many things to point out for orientation: the time, the day and date, the weather, the location of various items in the room, the orientation of the bed, the color of the gown, and the name of the nurse. Grounding in terms of being oriented to surroundings may be one of the first things a non-communicative patient loses, and the chaplain can provide some context.

Some other considerations

What about touching the patient?

Once the nurse or another member of the medical team tells you that the patient is stable enough to be touched by others, then it is up to your own comfort level and cultural awareness. An example of touch would be to extrapolate from the nurse's lead during the shadowing exercise:

- "Mrs. Jane, I am going to put my hand on your right hand for a moment."

- "Dr. Robert, I am going to place my hand on your left shoulder to let you know I am with you."

- "George, I am standing at the side of your bed, on your left side."

Voice of the Chaplain:

How long to stay?

Stay for as long as you are feeling a connection to the patient. The sense of connection may feel different with this person. You might be able to tolerate the circumstances for a few minutes. Try to stay just a little longer than what you can tolerate, so as to allow your own spirit to settle and be available. Some chaplains will find that the patient's spirit is more easily experienced than with someone who communicates with voice, eyes, or body movements. This is a chance to further expand your ability to be still, be with, tolerate, and relax.

When it is time to leave, say goodbye.

Wait—what about prayer?

That is its own topic in Chapter 7.

3

The Family Is Here

Balancing a Pastoral Visit with the Patient and the Family or Friends

Do not veil the truth with falsehood, nor conceal the truth knowingly.

The Quran 2:42

At first glance, it is a relief to learn there is family in the room with a non-communicative patient. There is someone who can describe the patient, and someone who will be in dialogue. While the team in the hallway may wonder about how the chaplain is able to interact in a room alone with a comatose patient, the chaplain is really in control of the general situation. We can take our time, listen, watch, be still, and notice. Family or friends in the room add a new dimension, as the chaplain must now balance time and attention as well as model an interactive behavior with a non-interactive patient.

Chaplains model behavior all the time. Some of this modeling has been part of our training and it is an everyday activity. For example, when we speak with staff or team about a patient or about their own concerns, we demonstrate non-judgmental listening and unconditional caring. We demonstrate our multilingual abilities as we seek out and use the most appropriate language of spirituality or emotional understanding. We dig into our built-in personal dictionaries and archives to offer texts or individual words or resources to patients, family, and staff to help them express themselves and to help them feel heard or seen. We are witnesses to the daily lives of the people surrounding us, and we hold what they give us.

Voice of the Chaplain:

I hate being spoken for, so I feel bad letting family speak for the patient.

In a room with family and a patient who cannot participate, we are faced with choices:

- Do I introduce myself first to the family and then to the patient?

- How do I help the family tell their story while making sure they know we do not discount the possibility that the patient could have some processing capacity?

- Where do I stand or sit?

- Who is the primary focus of the visit? When do I speak with the family? When with the patient?

- How do I include the patient in the conversation?

- What if the family is saying "she"? How do I model adjusting to "Jane"?

And we are faced with the imperative to respect and maintain the dignity and humanity of each person in the room.

ChapTime 7

Which of the above choices (also discussed further, below) is the most challenging to you? Consider how you might meet the challenge directly. Be bold.

Family and friends will have several dominating fears while in the room with the patient, and without asking we cannot know which are the greatest. (And asking must be done with the understanding that the patient can hear, so stepping outside the room can be helpful.) Experience will tell us that the fears include that the patient will remain in this non-communicative state, that the patient's wishes are unknown or are different from those of the proxy or surrogate, that the patient is suffering, that the patient's recovery will be only partial, and that the patient will die. Some visitors will, of course, want to introduce the chaplain to the patient, but many will be unclear about the chaplain's role or about how to interact with the patient.

Do I introduce myself to the family and then to the patient?

- "Good morning! I am Chaplain Greg and I saw you in the hallway before. May I come in and visit with you and Ms Jones? I want to introduce myself to Ms Jones so she knows who has come in to see her."

- "Hello! My name is Jen and I am the chaplain here today. The social worker suggested I come over to introduce myself as part of the team looking after Mr. Green. I wanted to let you know I have been visiting with Mr. Green the last several days, standing with him for a few minutes and letting him know about the weather and time of day. How are you all connected?"

- "Good evening! I am Sister Ellen and I am the chaplain for this ICU. I spent some time in conversation with Joanne a few days before her surgery. She spoke about her work and her family. Her nurse told me you were here now and I wanted to come say hello to her and to meet you at the same time."

How do I help the family tell their story while making sure they know we do not discount the possibility that the patient could have some processing capacity?

- "This sounds like quite a complex story. I wonder how much of it Ms Jones already knows. I am sure you already know we believe patients can hear us; we just don't know what they hear until they can tell us. Can we step to the door?"

- "It seems like you and your husband, Mr. Green, have been through a lot together to arrive at this place. What do you imagine him saying to you now?"

- "Maybe that's something you would like to say to Joanne directly. We can stand next to her together, if you like. It's ok to take her hand, to touch her, to let her know you are here. Also, I see Joanne's right foot is out from under the covers—does she like to have her feet massaged? You could do that, too."

Where do I stand or sit?

This is one of the eternal problems in a hospital room! Depending on the topic: either right next to the patient, inviting the visitors to join you, or at one end of the room with the visitors.

Who is the primary focus of the visit? When do I speak with the family? When with the patient?

Although this will depend on what prompted you to enter the room, it is critical to this venture of providing pastoral care to non-communicative patients that the patient always be included in the visit. Sometimes the visitors will not want to talk at all and you may find there is an awkward transition to then speaking directly to the patient, but this is your moment—go ahead. Remember that a visitor may not know how to connect to the loved one in the bed but you do, and you can model behavior. For example:

> "Ms Jones, this is Chaplain Greg. I am here with Jim and Jan, who are visiting. We were just talking about the fact that you may not realize you are in the hospital and that there are lots of machines and tubes all around. Your room faces the hallway and your nurses and doctors see you all the time. Your nurse today is Allison. You are in great and caring hands. Jim and Jan were also telling me about your children, and I have asked them to bring in some photographs of you and them so we can get to know you a bit."

How do I include the patient in the conversation?

You want to help the visitors teach you about the patient and what kinds of interests or activities she or he has. One of the gifts of pastoral care is to help people remember who they are when they are not in the hospital, and this includes the visitors. It is very challenging for family and friends to sit with a non-communicative patient, trying to work out how to connect, or how to sit quietly and share the space despite the noise and worry. Again you can model behavior. For example:

> "Mr. Green, your wife tells me you love newspaper editorials and short stories and that you both love choral music. Mrs. Green, I wonder if you would enjoy reading aloud a little to your husband? And I will look for a CD of choral music for you, or perhaps you have some favorite recordings."

Voice of the Chaplain:

Self-conscious in front of the family—are they judging me?

Voice of the Chaplain:

It feels like I am not doing enough.

What if the family is saying "she"? How do I model adjusting to "Jane"?

- "Please tell me—what name shall I use for your mother? I want to be sure to use the name your mother prefers, and to tell the medical team as well."

- "And do you call her Mom or Mother?"

- "It helps all of us, especially your mother, to call her by her name. It helps to orient her during this time."

4

The Team Will
See You Now

A Member of the Medical Team
Is in the Room or Nearby

We do not see things as they are. We see things as we are.

Rabbi Shmuel ben Nachmani, Talmudic tractate *Berakhot* 55b

Chaplains have expressed concern that members of the medical team will not immediately understand a pastoral visit with a non-communicative patient who is alone in a room—why not wait for the family? In the ICU there is often a loud voice trying to awaken comatose patients, to activate their bodies and bring them back to the surface of consciousness. Nurses and doctors will affirm that a patient may well hear the sound of voices, and there are studies and papers addressing the ability of the brain of a comatose patient to distinguish commands.[1]

---

1   Rohaut, B., Eliseyev, A., and Claassen, J. (2019) 'Uncovering Consciousness in Unresponsive ICU Patients: Technical, Medical and Ethical Considerations.' *Critical Care 23*, 1, 78.

ChapTime 8

How will you make your chaplain's voice heard?

During training, hospital chaplains find themselves in a range of unfamiliar and sometimes dramatic circumstances. The training is designed to help chaplains notice and manage their own responses to the surrounding stress in order to stay emotionally present and available to deliver spiritual care and support. A significant area of concern reported by chaplains is a sense of self-consciousness at being watched by the medical team.

Voice of the Chaplain:

I feel self-conscious when I'm with a non-responsive patient and a doctor, nurse, aide, or physical therapist comes into the room.

Chaplains work at the edges of the mainstream of hospital healthcare, sometimes experiencing an invisibility similar to that expressed by patients. At the same time, chaplains are highly exposed as we make our visits in glass-enclosed or barely private rooms or waiting areas. The chaplain learns to carve out a private space in the midst of the public arena of the hospital in an effort to respect the privacy and dignity of the patient and/or family, but also to give ourselves some protection from intrusion.

If professional chaplains want to continue building relationships with the medical team and increase the integration of spiritual care into the healing process, we need to be intentional about demonstrating and making tangible aspects of the work of pastoral care. An invitation into our work creates a cross-disciplinary model to help reduce both unfamiliarity for the team and self-consciousness for the chaplain. And asking to follow a member of the medical team, as we do with the nurses in the didactic, models the respect we are seeking for our own work. Shadowing and debriefing, demonstrating leadership in team or family meetings, collaborating on projects, leading grand rounds, and teaching in all forms are ways the chaplain can reach and actively include members of the care team in our work.

One of the steps we took to bring a medical team in the room with us, if only virtually, was through a PowerPoint presentation about pastoral care with non-communicative patients titled "What Are You Doing in There?" The audience laughter at seeing the title slide was partly in recognition of the medical team's own (sometimes unspoken) question. Bringing this unspoken question into the open and giving it voice is a significant part of this endeavor of spiritual care with non-communicative patients. The medical team and the chaplain raise the same concerns: "What *am* I doing in there? How *do* I explain it? How do I reduce *my* feelings of self-consciousness?"

Voice of the Chaplain:

Am I taking time away from medical care?

ChapTime 9

What concerns do you have about visiting a non-communicative patient when there is a member of the team already in the room?

There are professional courtesies to be observed, just as we expect for ourselves, and there is an excellent opportunity to see and be seen, to collaborate as appropriate to the circumstances. Perhaps the physical or respiratory therapist has met the family and can engage with the patient and you. Maybe the nurse has some information to share with the patient and you can be part of receiving and witnessing. Or the chaplain may have background to share with the other professionals in the room. Sometimes the chaplain's role is to introduce the people in the room to the patient.

5 | Staying in the Room

Drawing on Pastoral Skills to Stay until the Visit Is Complete

Wait for that wisest of all counselors, Time.

From *Plutarch's Lives*, Pericles, sec 18

Chaplains learn to develop a range of arcs in pastoral visits with interactive patients. These arcs are learned through debriefing the results of trial and error. There are the very short arcs in early training when we are relieved to be released quickly from a room, or glad to perform a task ("Oh no thank you, Chaplain, I am fine. But you could go see my neighbor, who is in bad shape?" "Please pray for me," "Are you the social worker? I need to see the social worker," "Can you get me a blanket?" or "Is there a Catholic priest here?" or a rabbi, an imam or a Russian Orthodox priest). In time, the chaplain becomes adept at taking the short arc and bending it to see if there is more as we learn to stay in the room. Longer arcs are made from patient responses including "Am I dying?" "I am not religious," "I am an atheist," "Who sent you?" or "Are you the one with the coloring books?"—leading the chaplain to help the patient access or re-access resources and resilience to tell the story of hope, meaning, and connection that needs to be told. Or the chaplain helps the patient to reveal a lack of resource or resilience, and make space for the isolation or hopelessness to surface in dialogue, telling the story of loss and sadness and everything in between.

ChapTime 10

Recall a visit when you were relieved to be
released from the room. See if you can bring up the
emotions you experienced; What are they?

When a pastoral visit is interrupted by the arrival of the care team or
a family member the chaplain must decide whether to keep going, to
break and return, to stop, or to bring the new person up to speed with
the visit. With an interactive patient there is a good chance that we will
be able to stay somewhat on track and re-capture the energy or find
new energy in the dialogue. The chaplain develops an intuitive sense
for what is going to be most productive, testing that intuition in each
encounter to strengthen it.

ChapTime 11

Recall a visit when you resisted the urge to be released and appropriately stood your ground, using your pastoral authority.

The interactive patient provides verbal and non-verbal cues to let the chaplain know to continue, to close, or to ask about whether or not to continue. Sometimes cues are a result of the medical circumstances of the patient (very talkative, lethargic, physically unsettled) and sometimes they signal "This is enough for now" (crossed arms, turning away, avoiding eye contact, looking at the phone). The chaplain is in an ongoing connection and dialogue with an interactive patient even if communication is compromised. Everything is different with a non-communicative patient. Or is it?

How will a non-responsive patient signal to you that the visit is welcome or not? How will you know when it is time to close the visit? These questions have been raised by every cohort of chaplains entering the didactic outlined earlier.

This guidebook is the result of a firm belief that once a patient is being cared for in the hospital setting, the chaplain is part of that care team. And further, that the ability to be in a pastoral relationship with a non-communicative patient is at the very heart of our pastoral skills: the ability to be still and be with someone without dialogue.[1] The skill of active silence is certainly worth being practiced with interactive patients as a respite from the onslaught of questions from the medical team, family, and friends, and it will bring satisfaction in visits with our non-responsive patients.

---

1   Psalm 46:10; 1 Kings 19:12 "still, small voice"

A warm-up exercise to use before entering the ICU

Sit with a partner and take turns only listening
and only speaking for 90 seconds.

Choose an open-ended question with some weight.
(When did you first become aware of your own mortality?
What gives you the greatest hope in your daily life? etc.)

The listener does not speak except to acknowledge
hearing the speaker. The speaker speaks to be heard.

Switch listener and speaker seamlessly, without conversation.

Now debrief:

Was the 90 seconds short or long?

How was it for the speaker to be heard
without commentary or interruption?

How was it for the listener to listen without
planning answers or giving advice?

What were the body sensations, the emotional
sensations, the spiritual experience?

Other observations:

Behaviors to cultivate

Let's now look at specific behaviors to cultivate and practice to help stay in the room with a non-communicative patient.

Presence

This is the practical beginning of the visit to a non-communicative patient, alone in the room. The Latin origin *praesentia* means "being at hand." Presence is a cultivated and constantly evolving behavior for the chaplain. It shifts in response to the needs of the patient. Who are you when you enter the patient's room? Who are you while you are at the bedside?

The chaplain's presence is active and engaged, grounded and resilient in the room of a non-communicative patient. When standing near the head of the patient's bed, you are quite literally at the hand of the patient and beginning to connect.

Stillness

Consider the difference between still water and sparkling water and locate yourself on the continuum between the bubbles and the still surface. The detail of the patient's condition is largely unknown, but if he or she is not communicative, not interactive, it would be reasonable to take the position that the patient is more still than bubbly. The chaplain enters the room from the socialized bubble that is outside the room and must adjust to match the more still surface inside to find a starting point for the connection. The adjustment can include taking a slow breath as you enter the room; slowing to the patient's tempo or matching the patient's ventilator-paced breathing; and slowing the pace of your steps to make it easier to take in the room as you enter. The purpose of this stilling is to feel the floor beneath your feet, to open and use your senses.

Sight

Consider how finely the body is made. Look at each visible part of the patient's body, beginning with the top of the head. See the shape, any bumps or scars, the way the hair grows (or doesn't) and its color, the eyebrows framing the bridge of the nose, the eyes and eyelashes, the movement of the eyes behind the eyelids, and the color of the eyes, if open. Take in the shape of the ears, the nose and cheeks, the jawbone, teeth, chin. Linger at any one or several of these long enough to know you have seen them. Continue to the neck, upper chest, arms, hands, fingers, shins, feet, toenails, etc. in the same fashion. These visible and distinctive parts of the body tell a story—smooth, tight, dry, or rough skin, clear or bruised, shaved, colored hair, tattoos, nail beds. Don't forget the gown, sheets, covers, and medical equipment and how they are arranged and connected.

Hearing

Learn the sounds of the machines and what they mean so they become part of the conversation rather than only interruptions—the ventilator, the shifting of the bed to prevent bed sores, the inflation and deflation of leg cuffs, and the bells, beeps, and sirens. Hear the buzzing in the hallway outside the room, and the muffled or loud sounds. Locate the hum in the room; the rush of air from the vent; the rattle of blinds against the window; the sound of the television, radio, or a CD (these might indicate something about the patient, the visitors, or the nurses). Notice people entering or leaving the room. Perhaps there is no sound, just silence. This auditory information creates the environment in which the patient is suspended. Find yourself suspended in the same environment.

Voice of the Chaplain:

There is a need to improvise around the machinery in the room.

Smell

There is no denying that hospital rooms smell of human waste. They also smell of aromatherapy patches, cleaning compounds, cologne, talcum powder, medications, food, adhesives, gauze, singed hair, lotion, homelessness. What about your patient? Is there a story to be extracted from the smells in the patient's room? What does it take for you to tolerate or incorporate the smells?

Touch

Why touch a non-communicative patient? Because the person is probably not being touched as much as when she or he was interactive, and the lack of daily touch contributes to isolation.[2] That being said, touch is subjective and personal. Each chaplain and each chaplain's training supervisor has their own view about touch. If you are ready to touch your non-communicative patient, make sure the nurse confirms that the patient is medically stable enough. Touching any part of the body is touching skin, and skin senses four major stimuli—pressure, temperature, pain, and vibration.[3]

Because we do not know the kind of touch preferred by a patient we must be especially mindful. (If there is a religious or cultural question, do not touch.) Assuming there is a clear path, an easy and appropriate way to touch a patient is to touch a hand, speaking as you do so: "Ms Jones, I am putting my hand on your right hand for a few moments." Feel your patient's skin and body temperature and notice if this changes anything in the patient or in you: heartbeat, body temperature, breathing rate, and emotional or spiritual state? Slowly take your hand away, letting your patient know as you move.

2   Abbas, M., Mohammadi, E., and Sheaykh Rezayi, A. (2009) 'Effect of a regular family visiting program as an affective, auditory, and tactile stimulation on the consciousness level of comatose patients with a head injury.' *Japan Journal of Nursing Science 6*, 1, 21–26.

Tjepkema-Cloostermans, M.C., Wijers, E.T., and van Putten, M.J.A.M. (2016) Stimulus induced bursts in severe postanoxic encephalopathy. *Clinical Neurophysiology 127*, 11, 3492–3497.

3   www.interactive-biology.com/3629/7-senses-and-an-introduction-to-sensory-receptors

ChapTime 12

Name the physical, emotional, and spiritual connections you feel.

And stay just a little longer.

Voice of the Chaplain:

For whom am I making this visit?

6

The Spiritual Heart of the Visit

How to Discover It

Let your life speak.

Quaker saying

A definition of just what is spiritual or what animates a person is timely here. It might include that which provides meaning and purpose in a life, or what gives a person the fullest sense of being human, the feeling of "Ah, I am in the right place; I know who I am and my purpose." While these can be applied to the chaplain in the room with the non-communicative patient, or family and friends, or the medical team, they cannot guide us to the spirit of the patient.

A non-communicative patient on life support has breathing, heart rate, and blood pressure controlled by a combination of machines and medications. Lines and numbers on the monitor screens are confirmations that the combination is meeting set targets rather than a sign of the physical body working in an integrated fashion. The visible signs of life are mechanically induced, and we cannot know what is going on inside the patient's mind or where the spirit might be located. And yet the chaplain is in the room looking to connect with the spiritual being, the person in the patient in the bed.

Voice of the Chaplain:

Sharing space with people, even in silence.

ChapTime 13

What about non-communicative patients who are not on life-support machines? How might that impact the chaplain's choice about how to connect?

Let's trace an overview of previous pages to bring the spiritual heart of the visit into greater focus. The chaplain enters the room as a witness to the patient's condition: an engaged, sensing, and perceiving witness rather than a spectator or signatory. You are a witness to the possibility of transcendence, of something beyond the regular human experience. You enter the room modeling the trust, the faith, that there is a vitality within the body of the patient and that you will connect with that vitality.

What if the spiritual heart of this pastoral visit is not a destination but rather the entire visit from the moment you enter the room? What if the act of crossing the threshold puts you in direct contact with the patient's spirit as it fills the room?

ChapTime 14

Identify three times you experienced the patient's spirit at the door to the room.

You have watched, looked, and listened; you have sat and stood with your patients, you have kept still. You are working to overcome the initial concerns that kept you out of the room. The connections you have experienced and named are key to discovering the spiritual in your visit with a non-communicative patient. We can learn about the physical, emotional, and social by observation and in conversation with others. The spiritual, however, we must learn ourselves by engaging with the person in the bed regardless of others in the room.

Voice of the Chaplain:

Trust that there is always more going on than meets the eye.

Chaplains are trained to work simultaneously at conscious and unconscious, or intuitive, levels to hear the spiritual aspects emerging from an interactive patient's presentation. When the patient cannot be in any traditional kind of dialogue, the chaplain must focus even more closely to become aware of the smallest sense of the spiritual to help fill in the fullness of the person in the bed. Neither verbal nor non-verbal behaviors will help this time. We gradually let go the drive for the rational and let the unspoken exchange shape into a meaningful spiritual exchange.

ChapTime 15

What are the spiritual aspects of visits with your non-communicative patients? Push yourself to identify the simplest and truest answer.

There are many ways to identify spiritual connection even amid the cacophony and visual chaos of the hospital ICU: the stillness or hush in the room, a deep sadness or joy, a reduction in extraneous noise in the mind, a sense of suspended time, self-consciousness turning into self-awareness, an increased focus outside of the self, a tingle.

ChapTime 16

How would you describe the sensation of a spiritual connection?

The pastoral caregiver's expertise in concentrated listening and watching is critical to being a trustworthy witness. Certainly, other care providers witness through presence and perception, but it is the pastoral caregiver's strength to experience and reflect on the sense of spirit in the room.

ChapTime 17

Identify texts from your religious or spiritual tradition and/or secular literature that strengthen your ability to experience and reflect on the sense of spirit in the room.

ChapTime 18

Name at least five examples of full humanity and personhood you have witnessed when visiting a non-communicative patient.

7 | Prayer

Every Step Is a Prayer

But we will give ourselves continually to prayer.

Acts 6:4

Finally, you say, we are going to pray. But why, and on whose account?

For a pastoral caregiver, prayer often implies an overt religious or spiritual dimension as we reach out to someone or something greater than ourselves. The urge to reach out in prayer arises from different places in the chaplain's heart, ranging from the practical (time to summarize the visit with a closing prayer) to the intuitive (a sense that a pause is needed so the patient feels heard and invited to speak more deeply). It can come from the chaplain's desire to reduce the tension in the room, to bring people together, to settle the unsettled, to collect urgent energy and direct it outwards.

The purpose of prayer is equally varied: to offer surrender; to summon strength, love, forgiveness, or grace; to connect with a religious or spiritual tradition; to feel less alone. In the hospital, bedside prayer often expresses directly what the patient hints at but is too fearful or worried or embarrassed to say aloud. Prayer can create a pause in the emotions in the room and open the door to the next part of a conversation.

How does this speak to the circumstances of a non-communicative patient, alone in a room, whose interest in prayer is unknown? Certainly, it is possible that the family has asked the chaplain to pray with them in the room with the patient or away from the room, or given permission to pray in the room if they are not present. Perhaps we knew the patient before she or he became non-communicative and we have a sense of a prayer life or desires. It is critical to the full dignity of the non-communicative patient to carefully consider the purpose of prayer and to be mindful about who is requesting it.

What about the icons, Bibles, electric Shabbat candles, rosaries, statues, ritual items, or prayer cards in the room? They might indicate the patient's expressions of beliefs or values but they could just as easily express the concerns and interests of visitors. What can the pastoral caregiver offer that might be considered a prayer or offering? For the non-communicative patient, each step of a chaplain's visit is certainly prayer in action—an offering from the chaplain's humanity to the patient's humanity. It may be enough to consider your intentional presence as a prayer.

But what if you have the thoughtful urge to make the kind of prayer that is an invocation, a request, a supplication or petition, a crying-out, a benediction or blessing? There are many ways to satisfy this urge that arises from the interaction with your patient. You could speak aloud a desire for the patient's healing or for comfort, or hum or sing a wordless melody; you might meditate. If you feel the need to speak more traditionally prayerful words, please consider this an opportunity to refill your own spiritual reservoir, stepping out of the room and enjoying the relief the prayer brings you.

ChapTime 19

Prepare three short examples of what you have said in the room of a non-communicative patient.

ChapTime 20

Given our travels together, prepare three short examples of what you might now consider saying.

Summary of Skills

What are some of the specific skills you observed or learned?

Please use this space to identify the skills you now have available to you. The information you include in these pages will serve as reminders and as building blocks for your continued learning.

Resources

The didactic
Introduction to the session

The leader begins by outlining the next two hours—pre-visit questionnaire, shadowing nurses, role plays, discussion, post-visit questionnaire, reflections, and closing. For evaluation purposes, it is helpful to have the pre-visit questions on the front of a piece of paper and the post-visit questions on the back. It is important to state up front that all questions and concerns will be delayed unless they are practical matters. This will help contain and focus the students' energy.

Pre-visit Questionnaire

This is filled out and each student marks their questionnaire with name or initials. The questionnaires are then collected, to be returned at the end of the didactic for the second set of questions. It is helpful for the leader to review the initial responses to make sure that concerns are addressed in action or in conversation.

Please fill this in for yourself as you begin to work with this guidebook.

Pre-visit Questionnaire

What kinds of general concerns do you have when visiting with a non-communicative patient?

When visiting non-communicative patients with family present?

Without family present?

In the intensive care unit (ICU)

The students wanted an in-hospital, hands-on, witnessed experience rather than a classroom lecture. Who better to demonstrate how to communicate with non-responsive patients than the ICU nurses who spend long hours getting to know their patients, often without benefit of information from family or friends? As noted earlier, the nurses were at first uncomfortable but then delighted, forthcoming, shy, and uncertain, just like the students. They happily modeled the ways in which they addressed and spoke to their patients, what they talked about, the tone of voice used, and the details of location or nursing care being given. If the patient is on isolation, there is also a chance to help the chaplains chip away at the barriers raised by putting on gowns and gloves. The students are asked to stand close to the nurse and the patient, silently observing and saving questions for outside the room. The chaplain students are for the most part very engaged, although occasionally frightened or stressed by what they see or feel in the room.

Ideally the students shadow two different nurses, seeing two or three patients. Sometimes there is family present, sometimes not. The most difficult part of the didactic is setting up the visits. The ICU is a dynamic setting and a patient who was comatose in the morning may have awoken by the afternoon, or the medical needs of the unit may have shifted dramatically. The didactic leader needs to be flexible and creative.

It is worth noting that an unexpected by-product of these sessions is the active integration of chaplains onto a unit. The connection made between the nurses and the chaplains as the nurses are witnessed doing their work makes it easier for the chaplains to be witnessed doing theirs.

The role play

Following the sessions with the ICU nurses the students are given one of several scenarios depending on the number of students in the group. The role play is to build on the witnessed experience in the ICU to help the students embody it. The scenario roles include a non-communicative patient, a nurse, a chaplain, and family, and the students choose their roles. The student playing the patient must keep eyes closed and be in at least a semi-reclining position. The other students flesh out their roles according to the scenario. The duration of the role play depends on the students, and the leader may need to coach or even coax until there is a natural stopping place. Each student then reports the experience of the role play, with the student-patient going last. Several sample role plays are included in this Resources section, and you are encouraged to create role plays with specific connections to your student and patient populations.

Post-visit Questionnaire

The original questionnaire is returned to the students so they can answer the follow-up questions.

Post-visit Questionnaire

What are some of the specific skills you observed or learned?

Were there spiritual aspects to these visits?
If so, please elaborate.

What are the remaining obstacles?

Additional feedback:

The questionnaires are collected for program evaluation. A selection of responses to both sections of the questionnaire can be found in the Voice of the Chaplain, throughout this guidebook and at the back of the Resources section.

Closing discussion and reflection

This is a time for any additional thoughts, emotions, and questions to be raised. On some visits, students will find themselves surprised by what they witnessed in a nurse's interactions with the patient or family. Or they may find that the intensity of the role play raised additional questions. Closing the didactic with a prayer or poem or breathing can help seal the work.

Evaluation

Review the collected questionnaires to check the learning and to adjust the didactic. A short follow-up with the group of students after several weeks is helpful to all concerned.

ChapTime reflections

ChapTime 1

Recall a conversation when you were told you did not need to visit a comatose patient because he or she would not be able to engage with you. How did you feel?

ChapTime 2

Stand still. Which sounds go with which piece of medical machinery?

ChapTime 3

What is the story being told by bedside monitors? What is the tone of the conversations around you? Any smells? What do you think? How do you feel?

ChapTime 4

What concerns do you have about visiting a non-communicative patient?

ChapTime 5

What expectations of yourself do you carry in the moment of entering a patient's room? And when standing in the room?

ChapTime 6

Consider the items that would help a care team begin to get to know you if you were the patient.

ChapTime 7

Which of the choices outlined in Chapter 3 is the most challenging to you? Consider how you might meet the challenge directly. Be bold.

ChapTime 8

How will you make your chaplain's voice heard?

ChapTime 9

What concerns do you have about visiting a non-communicative patient when there is a member of the team already in the room?

ChapTime 10

Recall a visit when you were relieved to be released from the room. See if you can bring up the emotions you experienced.

ChapTime 11

Recall a visit when you resisted the urge to be released and appropriately stood your ground, using your pastoral authority.

ChapTime 12

Name the physical, emotional, and spiritual connections you feel.

ChapTime 13

What about non-communicative patients who are not on life-support machines. How might that impact the chaplain's choice about how to connect?

ChapTime 14

Identify three times you experienced the patient's spirit at the door to the room.

ChapTime 15

What are the spiritual aspects of visits with your non-communicative patients? Push yourself to identify the simplest and truest answer.

ChapTime 16

How would you describe the sensation of a spiritual connection?

ChapTime 17

Identify texts from your religious or spiritual tradition and/or secular literature that strengthen your ability to experience and reflect on the sense of spirit in the room.

ChapTime 18

Name at least five examples of full humanity and personhood you have witnessed when visiting a non-communicative patient.

ChapTime 19

Prepare three short examples of what you have said in the room of a non-communicative patient.

ChapTime 20

Given our travels together, prepare three short examples of what you might now consider saying.

Role plays

The members of the group can either volunteer for a role in the role play or draw a slip of paper denoting their role. It is helpful to give each participant a copy of the role play (the ones below or others of your own devising) and to read it aloud. You can give the participants a few minutes to organize themselves and their relationships and to answer any immediate concerns that may be raised. The role plays are meant to be hands-on, instructive, possibly fun, possibly volatile. The leader of the group will need to make sure the scenario is moving along and reassure the players that conflict is appropriate. The leader will also need to close the role play at an appropriate time. The usual duration is approximately ten minutes. The debrief of the players' experience can be in any order so long as the person playing the non-communicative patient goes last.

Role Play A: In the ICU, following a brain bleed

The chaplain receives a referral from the social worker for patient Alice Warner, without any information about religious affiliation or background. Ms Warner appears to be middle-aged; the room is full of medical machinery. There are no personal items. Ms Warner is lying in bed, intubated, sedated, with her eyes closed.

Ms Warner's nurse is in the room and tells the chaplain that the patient arrived in the middle of the night from an outside hospital following a brain bleed.

(What is the interaction between the chaplain, the nurse, and the patient?)

Two or more people are standing outside the room, observing what is going on in the room.

(How might the interaction between the chaplain, the nurse, and the patient continue?)

These people turn out to be family and they enter the room. They stand on either side of the bed and begin to ask questions and to talk about the patient as if she is not present.

(How does the chaplain respond?)

The nurse excuses him- or herself to care for another patient.

The family members have received an unclear prognosis for Ms Warner's recovery and they begin to speak about their concerns, talking over the patient.

(What is the interaction between the chaplain, the family, and the patient?)

The visit concludes.

Roles required

Alice Warner, the patient: Non-speaking role, but following the role play will report any experiences and/or sensations (spiritual, physical, emotional).

Chaplain: Speaking role.

Nurse: Speaking role; decide in advance if it will be all right for the chaplain to touch the patient.

Family Members: Speaking roles; please decide the relationship to the patient and each other.

Role Play B: In the ICU, following heart transplant surgery

The chaplain receives a referral for Alice Warner. There is no information about religious affiliation, and she appears to be middle-aged. She is intubated and sedated. The nurse, who is in the room, tells the chaplain that the patient has been this way for two days, following a heart transplant. It is the nurse who made the referral.

(What is the interaction between the chaplain, the nurse, and the patient?)

Two or more family members enter the room and stand on either side of the bed. They begin to speak over the patient, calling her "she." The nurse excuses her- or himself to care for another patient and leaves the room.

(How does the chaplain respond?)

The family members have been given an unclear prognosis for Ms Warner, the patient. They begin to talk about her and her prognosis.

(How does the chaplain interact with the family and the patient?)

The visit concludes.

Roles required

Alice Warner, the patient: Non-speaking role, but following the role play will report any experiences and/or sensations (spiritual, physical, emotional).

Chaplain: Speaking role.

Nurse: Speaking role; decide in advance if it will be all right for the chaplain to touch the patient.

Family Members: Speaking roles; please decide the relationship to the patient and each other.

Role Play C: The patient without visitors

The chaplain receives a referral from the unit assistant to visit Jack James, who recently underwent amputation of his left leg below the knee. Although unconfirmed, the unit assistant tells the chaplain she thinks that prior to the surgery she heard the patient indicate a connection to the Catholic Church. Mr. James is intubated and sedated. His nurse tells the chaplain that the patient had been agitated and he is now wearing protective mittens. His nurse also says that, in the four days since his surgery, he has had no visitors.

(How does the chaplain interact with the unit assistant, the nurse and the patient?)

Roles required

Jack James, the patient: Non-speaking role, but following the role play will report any experiences and/or sensations (spiritual, physical, emotional).

Chaplain: Speaking role.

Nurse: Speaking role (decide in advance if the chaplain can touch the patient).

Unit Assistant: Speaking role.

Voice of the Chaplain

Over the following pages are comments from the questionnaires given to each of the several hundred participants. The selections represent the most common concerns.

Pre-visit Questionnaire

What kinds of concern do you have when visiting non-communicative patients?

What is the most effective manner to begin the pastoral visit?

I might say or do something that, if the patient were awake, she or he might not like.

My greatest concern is feeling or looking silly as I interact with the non-responsive patients with an audience.

I feel self-conscious or awkward when I am with a non-responsive patient, and a doctor, nurse, aide, or physical therapist comes into the room.

Whose consent do I need before visiting?

Should I pray? Would the patient have wanted prayer if conscious?

I don't want to impose my own viewpoints or theologies.

Do I violate a patient's privacy by entering the room when she or he cannot indicate a desire for a visit?

How do I support patient autonomy when I don't know what she or he needs or wants?

What can I do other than pray or read scripture?

Are others watching or listening to me?

How long should I stay?

I am not sure I see the point in visiting with a non-communicative patient.

Are there responsive patients who need me more?

How do I know a patient's beliefs or values?

How do I connect with the patient?

What language do I speak?

There is no direct feedback from the patient.
How will I know if I have done a good job?

I don't like the energy in the ICU—how do I harden myself against
the edge of death and yet stay soft enough to open my heart?

How do I improvise around the machinery in the room?

When visiting non-communicative patients with family present?

I feel self-conscious in front of the family—are they judging me?

How will I focus the family on the patient rather
than on the information about the patient?

The rooms are so small and crowded.
How do I avoid talking over the patient?

The family sometimes speak about the patient as an absent
third party. Is it rude to encourage them to be more inclusive?

I hate being spoken for, and I am uncomfortable
when a family speaks for the patient.

Will my presence raise scary or painful thoughts?

Does my speaking directly to/with the patient
raise false hope in the family?

The visit never feels meaningful. I don't think I am doing anything.

What tense do I use when speaking about
the patient—past, present, future?

I am concerned that my tone of voice will irritate the family—
soothing rather than cheerleading.

Do I join with the family in their hope for a miracle?

Am I taking time away from medical care?

I don't want to feel like I am performing for the family.

The visit feels absurd, like an existential candid-camera episode.

Do the family accurately represent what the patient would want?

How do I invite the family outside the room to talk?

Without family present?

I don't go in. I don't understand why I should.

Is the patient maybe lonely?

For whom am I making this visit?

It is frustrating not being able to communicate.
Am I contributing to that frustration?

I am too uncomfortable to embrace the silence in the room.

How do I make the patient feel safe with me?

I need a role model.

Where do I look for the connection with the patient?

How do I know I have made a difference?

Overcoming the discomfort of thinking "Am I talking to myself?"

Post-visit Questionnaire

What are some of the specific skills you observed or learned?

It was intriguing to hear from nurses that they
actually talk to their unresponsive patients.

Tell the patient who you are and why you are in
the room; narrate what you are doing.

Make the assumption that the person is aware
and sentient even if they can't respond.

Be gentle.

Speak in order to create a sense of safety for the patient.

Touch is ok.

Encourage family to bring photos of the patient.

Use the same tone as with responsive patients,
not infantilizing or whispering.

Make direct statements rather than asking open-ended questions.

Be clear and succinct.

Treat the patient as you wish to be treated.

Stand close to the patient.

Don't overthink the visit—be as warm and kind as you usually are.

My senses were heightened.

Talk more to the nurses and doctors!

Use the patient's name.

Were there spiritual aspects to these visits? If so, please elaborate.

The patient is seen and treated as a full person, with dignity.

To spend regular time with a patient who does not respond
to one's presence in any visible way (even by heart rate)
is to trust, and even to quietly suggest to those witnessing,
that there is always more going on than meets the eye.

The most spiritual aspect of the visits was the evident caring that
the nurses had for their patients. It was clear that the nurses saw
their patients as full persons and not just as a body in a bed.

Offering pastoral care to non-responsive patients provides
an opportunity to uphold and value the personhood
of another, regardless of that person's incapacity
to express it either tangibly or in language.

In visiting with a non-communicative patient we affirm, and
experience ourselves, that there is more to a person than the
limitations of his/her body. To do so in a setting that focuses,
naturally, on the body's disability strikes me as profoundly spiritual.

I am reconsidering how I think about non-communicative
patients, granting them more awareness and humanity
than previously, and with more empathy.

Gentleness, human kindness, presence, and touch
are all expressions of spiritual connection.

Sharing space with people, even in silence.

Caring, companioning, connectedness.

The simple dignity of personhood.

What are the remaining obstacles?

The silence from the patient makes me feel the
patient's isolation and is anxiety-provoking.

There is no way to know what a patient wants or is experiencing.

Proceeding as though the patient can hear makes including
family members in the conversation more complicated.

Touch—I don't have language about my impulse to
touch in certain cases, except for a vague instinct
that it might be comforting. But for whom?

How do I make a spiritual assessment for a patient who
is unable to communicate? How do I plan spiritual
interventions with these patients? I do some of this work
intuitively, but how can I be more intentional?

How do I recover from a series of visits with
non-communicative patients?

How do I know if the patient is scared?
And do I need to even know?

The medical equipment makes the room
feel cramped and impersonal.

Overcoming the awkwardness of the circumstances.

Helping family or medical team adjust language or tone.

Moving the family conversation out of the room.

Family conflict at the bedside.

Do I have to speak the patient's language
or is the sound of a voice enough?

Trusting myself enough to know that my presence
and visit were of value to the patient.

Modeling for family that I am not fearful in the
presence of a non-communicative patient.

Creating peace with silence when the alarms are "speaking."

Further reading

Books

Awdish, Rana. *In Shock: My Journey from Death to Recovery and the Redemptive Power of Hope*. New York, NY: St. Martin's Press, 2017.

Boisen, Anton T. *Vision from a Little Known Country: A Boisen Reader*. Ed. Glenn H. Asquith. Decatur, GA: Journal of Pastoral Care Publications, 1992.

Boss, Pauline. *Ambiguous Loss: Learning to Live with Unresolved Grief*. Cambridge, MA: Harvard University Press, 1999.

Cooper-White, Pamela. *Shared Wisdom: Use of the Self in Pastoral Care and Counseling*. Minneapolis, MN: Fortress Press, 2004.

Doehring, Carrie. *The Practice of Pastoral Care: A Postmodern Approach*. Rev. and exp. edn. Louisville, KY: Westminster John Knox Press, 2015.

Frank, Arthur W. *The Wounded Storyteller: Body, Illness, and Ethics*. Chicago, IL: University of Chicago Press, 1995.

Friedman, Edwin H. *Friedman's Fables*. New York, NY: Guilford Press, 1990.

Gilligan, Carol. *In a Different Voice: Psychological Theory and Women's Development*. Cambridge, MA: Harvard University Press, 2016.

Kirkwood, Neville A. *A Hospital Handbook on Multiculturalism and Religion: Practical Guidelines for Health Care Workers*. Rev. edn. Harrisburg, PA: Morehouse Publishing, 2006.

Kushner, Harold S. *When Bad Things Happen to Good People*. 2nd edn. New York, NY: Schocken Books, 1989.

Lebacqz, Karen, and Joseph D. Driskill. *Ethics and Spiritual Care: A Guide for Pastors, Chaplains and Spiritual Directors*. Nashville, KY: Abingdon Press, 2000.

Matlins, Stuart M. and Arthur J. Magida (eds.) *How to Be a Perfect Stranger: The Essential Religious Etiquette Handbook*. 6th edn. Woodstock, VT: SkyLight Paths Publishing, 2015.

Nouwen, Henry J.M. *The Wounded Healer: Ministry in Contemporary Society*. New York, NY: Image, 1979.

O'Donohue, John. *To Bless the Space between Us: A Book of Blessings*. New York, NY: Doubleday, 2008.

Remen, Rachel N. *Kitchen Table Wisdom: Stories that Heal*. New York, NY: Riverhead Books, 1996.

Stairs, Jean. *Listening for the Soul: Pastoral Care and Spiritual Direction*. Minneapolis, MN: Fortress Press, 2000.

Taylor, Jill B. *My Stroke of Insight*. Penguin, 2009.

Ulanov, Ann B. *Finding Space: Winnicott, God, and Psychic Reality*. Louisville, KY: Westminster John Knox Press, 2001.

van der Kolk, Bessel. *The Body Keeps the Score: Brain, Mind, and Body in the Healing of Trauma*. New York, NY: Penguin, 2014.

Journal articles

Abbas, M., Mohammadi, E., and Sheaykh Rezayi, A. (2009) 'Effect of a regular family visiting program as an affective, auditory, and tactile stimulation on the consciousness level of comatose patients with a head injury.' *Japan Journal of Nursing Science* 6, 1, 21–26.

Eickhoff, S.B., Dafotakis, M., Grefkes, C., Stöcker, T., Shah, N.J., *et al.* (2008) 'fMRI reveals cognitive and emotional processing in a long-term comatose patient.' *Experimental Neurology 214*, 2, 240–246.

Fischer, D. and Truog, R.D. (2015) 'What is a reflex? A guide for understanding disorders of consciousness.' *Neurology 85*, 6, 543–548.

Frank, L. and Klincewicz, M. (2016) 'What does consciousness have to do with it? Quality of life in patients with disorders of consciousness.' *AJOB Neuroscience 7*, 1, 50–52,

Løvstad, M., Nyheim S., Kari, K., Marit, G., *et al.* (2018) '"It gets better. It can't be worse than what we have been through." Family accounts of the minimally conscious state.' *Brain Injury 32*, 13–14, 1659–1669.

Pistoia, F., Sacco, S., Stewart, J., Sarà, M., and Carolei, A. (2016) 'Disorders of consciousness: Painless or painful conditions?—Evidence from neuroimaging studies.' *Brain Sciences 6*, 4, 47.

Rohaut, B., Eliseyev, A., and Claassen, J. (2019) 'Uncovering Consciousness in Unresponsive ICU Patients: Technical, Medical and Ethical Considerations'. *Critical Care 23*, 1, 78.

Tjepkema-Cloostermans, M.C., Wijers, E.T., and van Putten, M.J.A.M. (2016) 'Stimulus induced bursts in severe postanoxic encephalopathy.' *Clinical Neurophysiology 127*, 11, 3492–3497.

Acknowledgements

There are many people who have supported the development of the didactic that then grew into this book. Thank you.

I want to highlight:

The nurses and the physicians in the Neuroscience and the Cardio-Thoracic Intensive Care Units at NewYork-Presbyterian/Columbia University Irving and Weill Cornell Medical Centers.

The clinical pastoral education interns and residents at NewYork-Presbyterian Hospital, and their program directors and educators the Reverend Dr. Beth Faulk Glover, Chaplain Leslie Kirzner, and Rabbi Naomi Kalish, for making it possible for us to develop and implement training on how to offer spiritual support to non-communicative patients.

Rabbi Mychal B. Springer for believing the didactic could be expanded to include the men and women living in the Mollie and Jack Zicklin Residence in Riverdale, and for her many years of steady mentoring.

Rabbi Daniel Silberbusch for implementing the didactic with his Pastoral Care Residents at NYP Brooklyn Methodist Hospital and proving that it could be replicated.

The Reverend Walter Dixon, who suggested the critical idea of the role play.

The New York Society Library for the shelter and resources required to write.

The Reverend Jose Maria Collazo, Lizzie Leiman Kraiem, and Alex Presciutti for reading the early drafts and offering ideas, most of which are included.

My tireless wife, Diane Wondisford, who reassured me that there really was a book in the first draft, and provided pastoral and emotional support that only a theater producer can offer.

Index